Fun on the Farm

AT THE
HORSE FARM

By Bruce Esseltine

Gareth Stevens
PUBLISHING

Please visit our website, www.garethstevens.com. For a free color catalog of all our high-quality books, call toll free 1-800-542-2595 or fax 1-877-542-2596.

Cataloging-in-Publication Data

Names: Esseltine, Bruce.
Title: At the horse farm / Bruce Esseltine.
Description: New York : Gareth Stevens Publishing, 2017. | Series: Fun on the farm | Includes index.
Identifiers: ISBN 9781482455243 (pbk.) | ISBN 9781482455267 (library bound) | ISBN 9781482455250 (6 pack)
Subjects: LCSH: Horses–Juvenile literature. | Horse farms–Juvenile literature.
Classification: LCC SF302 .E87 2017 | DDC 636.1–dc23

First Edition

Published in 2017 by
Gareth Stevens Publishing
111 East 14th Street, Suite 349
New York, NY 10003

Copyright © 2017 Gareth Stevens Publishing

Editor: Ryan Nagelhout
Designer: Laura Bowen

Photo credits: Cover, p. 1 Olga_i/Shutterstock.com; p. 5 Conny Sjostrom/Shutterstock.com; p. 7 Alexy Stiop/ Shutterstock.com; p. 9 (woman and horse) Darren Baker/Shutterstock.com; p. 9 (background) jessicakirsh/ Shutterstock.com; pp. 11, 24 (hay) jax973/Shutterstock.com; pp. 13, 24 Geza Farkas/Shutterstock.com; p. 15 Nicole Ciscato/Shutterstock.com; p. 17 risteski goce/Shutterstock.com; p. 19 Tim Platt/Iconica/ Getty Images; pp. 21, 24 (foal) everydoghasastory/Shutterstock.com; p. 23 Lasse Ansaharju/Shutterstock.com.

Printed in the United States of America

CPSIA compliance information: Batch #CW17GS: For further information contact Gareth Stevens, New York, New York at 1-800-542-2595.

Contents

Horses live on farms.
Farmers use horses
for work.

Some farms
only raise horses.
These are horse farms!

Farmers take good care of horses.

They feed horses hay.

They brush their hair!

13

Horses love to run.

They grow big
and strong.

Farmers often ride horses, too.

Some horses
have babies.
These are called foals.

21

Their moms are called dams.

Words to Know

brush

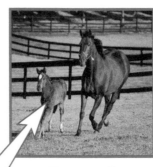
foal

hay

Index